LONDON CAFFS

For Lili, Ella and Kriszti and for all
those who keep the caffs going,
particularly at my local, the River Cafe.

LONDON CAFFS

Edwin Heathcote
Photography by Sue Barr

Published in Great Britain in 2004 by Wiley-Academy, a division of
John Wiley & Sons Ltd

Copyright © 2004   John Wiley & Sons Ltd, The Atrium, Southern
                     Gate, Chichester,
                     West Sussex PO19 8SQ, England
                     TelepNationalhone   01243 779777
                     International   (+44) 1243 779777

Photography © 2004 Sue Barr

This publication is designed to provide accurate and authoritative
information in regard to the subject matter covered. It is sold on the
understanding that the Publisher is not engaged in rendering professiona
services. If professional advice or other expert assistance is required, the
services of a competent professional should be sought.

Other Wiley Editorial Offices

John Wiley & Sons Inc., 111 River Street, Hoboken, NJ 07030, USA
Jossey-Bass, 989 Market Street, San Francisco, CA 94103-1741, USA
Wiley-VCH Verlag GmbH, Boschstr. 12, D-69469 Weinheim, Germany
John Wiley & Sons Australia Ltd, 33 Park Road, Milton, Queensland
4064, Australia
John Wiley & Sons (Asia) Pte Ltd, 2 Clementi Loop #02-01, Jin Xing
Distripark, Singapore 129809
John Wiley & Sons Canada Ltd, 22 Worcester Road, Etobicoke,
Ontario, Canada M9W 1L1ISBN 0470094389

Design: Christian K sters, CHK Design, London

Printed and bound in Italy by Conti Tipocolor

CONTENTS

FOREWORD

I started thinking about this book ten years ago and I should have written it then. This is probably as late as we could possibly leave it as the subject, the London caff, is dying. More than half the caffs on my original list had gone by the time of writing. Indeed I expect some of the entries in this book will not have survived until publication. This puts the book in the unusual position of having to fulfil a number of roles. The most important may well be as a visual document of a significant part of the city's streetscape and social history, and of an aesthetic moment. It has another role as a guidebook, a tool to help the reader navigate the remnants of London's caff culture. Its third role, the saddest, may well be as an obituary.

The London caff is so much a part of the city's public space – accessible, ubiquitous, cheap, unhurried – that I felt I should have been drawing some kind of Nolli plan with the interiors highlighted as extensions of the street. But the size of London prohibits any such exercise.

Sue Barr's wistful, often painfully poignant photos far better describe the atmosphere and look of the few surviving caffs than my text possibly could. Consequently I've largely confined myself to a neutral description of the caffs as manifestations of the ordinary. It is in this that the book departs most radically from the more usual architectural guide. Here, the object is not to find the beautiful, the bizarre or the extraordinary, but to identify the everyday: cafés that have become part of the fabric of the city, that melt into its steely-grey streets and sludge-coloured walls.

This is a brief study of an institution which is becoming defunct in the face of competition from national and international chains serving oversized and overpriced coffee, and where tea, the national drink, is reduced to a cipher of itself – a memory of a flavour represented by a bag in a cup of milky hot water. In the caff, the Italian immigrants adapted themselves to the primitive, undemanding culture of British food and created institutions that became synonymous with their locations, evolving as an indispensable part of the streets, the locales and the broader city. Italian café culture, in its homeland, is fast, fresh and varies hugely depending on which part of the country you are in. With the new coffee chains, Anglo-Saxons have reinvented it as a pre-packaged, self-service, themed experience – bland, universal and impermanent.

The aim of this book is to bring together a selection of some of the finest, and some of the most representative, surviving London caffs while it is still possible to document a selection of even this modest size. This may not be a fair representation: I have certainly left out good examples and put in a few bland ones. To make the book as usable and useful as possible (for tourists, walkers and flaneurs), I have concentrated on central London, even though there are many fine caffs on the outskirts and the peripheries, particularly at London's eastern extremities. My choice is biased towards the area I know best, the bit of London from Fulham to the West End. There is no attempt at fairness here, just a purely personal selection narrowed down and filtered through Sue Barr's lens. I hope the book proves useful in exploring the extraordinarily ordinary world of caffs and in documenting the dying gasps of working-class catering. Most of all, I hope it remains a useful guide and does not become an illustrated obituary.

Edwin Heathcote

INTRODUCTION

There is nothing that smells more of London than a caff. The increasingly sparse network of surviving refuges represents the dying, but still steaming, breath of a particular moment in the city's history. I use the word refuge carefully because once inside these stuffy, buzzy rooms, you are ensconced in a disappearing world sheltered from the latest fads, corporate gimmicks and design trends, sheltered from an alienating and increasingly alien culture of globalised and sterilised shopping, eating and consuming. Most of all, you are sheltered from pitiful illusions of a class-free society and the results of an attempt to homogenise the urban landscape and social hierarchy until the things that made us glad and proud to be alive have been ironed out. Caffs are not about lifestyle, they are about everyday life.

Although I am billed here as an architect and an architectural critic, I have resolutely not set out to write a book about architecture, and even less one about design. Neither have I attempted to write a book about food, a gastronomic guide. Nor is this book about conservation, about history or about a nostalgic yearning for a mythologised and idealised past. And it is not an ironic, postmodern style guide. It is simply an attempt to log and record some of the finest surviving examples of an institution which has been absolutely pivotal in forming modern London, the London that I have known and grown up with, and which remains fundamental in defining at least one facet of the city's character.

London, we often hear and read, has become the gastronomic capital of the world. We know this because we read it in London publications written by those who spend all their time eating extravagant free meals in the capital's finest restaurants. We read how, years ago, London was a culinary black hole, a disaster area of Brown Windsor and

overcooked greens. It was impossible to get a good cup of coffee. We read how wonderful it is that the corporate coffee chains have sprung up to save us with their wonderful coffee and qualified *baristas*. Where else could you have gone for a coffee and a chat?

The answer to this rhetorical question is important and illustrates a myopia that explains the gradual demise of London's unique café culture. The answer is that we used to go to the caff. The problem with the question, however, is that it is the wrong one. The actual, implied question is where did the middle classes go to lounge about and drink oversized cups of overpriced and overspecified coffee. The answer, as all the publications attest, is nowhere. The working classes, however, had no such problem. They went to the caff. They were accompanied there by a few bohos and stragglers who were uninterested in questions of class and were generally egalitarian, or who were self-consciously slumming it and enjoying their new surroundings, or who were oblivious to any connotations of class.

The caffs were, in many ways (both conscious and subconscious), what our present-day foodies and gastronomists, the chroniclers of greed and excessive consumption, were rebelling against and they represent everything that the gastro-industry is glad to see the back of. The menus are always the same and resolutely working class; this is the gastronomy of the council estate and the manual worker. It is a diet set out for physical work where the Full English Breakfast is a kind of Holy Grail of absolute sustenance, a meal which can make the grimmest and most backbreaking of jobs bearable. It is not the diet of the sedentary metropolitan elite. Yet, like it or not, it is also probably the city's most authentic and representative

meal and one which is very fine, appreciated by even the foreigners usually so dismissive of English cuisine.

The background to the animosity towards, contempt for, or at best blindness to, the culture of caffs is important because it is what is leading to their demise.

CAFFS: THE BACKGROUND

The caffs that concern us here are the result of a particular set of circumstances, trends and socio-economic conditions that defined London at a particular moment and which still embody the city's fundamental preoccupations and populations. These are almost all post-war institutions owned and run by Italian families. They stem from an era that was among the most deprived and miserable in the city's history yet which, paradoxically, also saw the establishment of the institutions fundamental to social welfare and the living standards that have been so effectively eroded over the last two decades.

Britain had participated in, and won, a war that saw it depleted financially, with a reduced male population. Success in the war came at a high price: the loss of the empire which had made the country, and particularly London, so fabulously wealthy; huge debts to the USA incurred from the sale of arms and supplies; and the lingering, seemingly never-ending curse of rationing. Good food was available only to those in the country whose tables were stocked from their own land, or those who could afford to resort to the burgeoning black market.

Italy too had been hit hard by the war and, despite an economic miracle in its industrial centres as the makers of arms switched to scooters and coffee machines, times in the smaller towns and villages were extraordinarily tough. An established and successful Italian community in Clerkenwell and a fast-growing second centre in Soho encouraged thousands of immigrants to settle in the capital immediately after the end of the war. Italians, as the cliché goes, really do love their food. So how did they end up making egg and chips, and endless cups of steaming tea? It is hard to imagine foods more alien to their sophisticated and highly regionalised gastronomical culture. Their counterparts who emigrated to New York and Chicago opened pizza joints and pasta restaurants, albeit serving meatballs with spaghetti and pizza pies with processed cheese, bastardising their cuisine to sell it to a hungry clientele.

The answer, I think, lies in a blend of opportunism, expedience and the wit to spot a gap in the market. As well, of course, as an innate culture of catering and service which was (and which remains) utterly alien to this island.

In London during this period, eating out was a middle-class conception. There were dining rooms, chop-houses and, later, milk bars which served a mix of lower-middle and working classes at relatively cheap prices. Of course there were pubs, but there was no equivalent of the caff. The dining rooms were the anachronistic leftovers of the Edwardian era, stiff, dark and uninviting. The chop-houses, although often very fine, were a remnant of an even earlier era and usually not particularly cheap – the meat rationing during and subsequent to the war put many out of business. The pubs were working class but they were, and still are, fundamentally about alcohol and getting drunk, totally unlike the bars of continental Europe. The milk bars, often established by teetotal and religious businessmen, retained something of that puritanism even through their often striking Art Deco designs. They were useful but not convivial.

London in the immediate post-war period, as photographs, films and inhabitants attest, was a dreary place, a city of browns and greys aesthetically stuck in the Edwardian era, where surfaces were relentlessly painted over in dun colours, where the working classes lived in the slums which had yet to be demolished, and where bomb sites broke the cityscape like a profile

of bad teeth. Art Deco, which had struck briefly during the previous decade, had left its glamorous mark in cinemas and hotels but had left the basic structure of the city alone. Most importantly, perhaps, the traditional class structure which had acted like a form of apartheid more strongly in this city than in any other in Europe or the USA, had begun to break down.

The war had brought the social classes together but the returning servicemen who had fought and saved their country from Nazism also returned with a bolshy attitude, an idea that they deserved better, replacing the more acquiescent, 'mustn't grumble' stance of their parents. This phenomenon was perfectly captured in Churchill's shock defeat in the general election of 1945, when an enormously popular war leader and hero was unceremoniously and mercilessly dumped because he was perceived to embody the values of an older world which had passed.

The radical programme of welfare reform embarked on by the victorious Labour government is also an indication of this spirit of change.

The Italian immigrants saw their opportunity. Whereas London's pubs and dining rooms made a virtue of their cosiness, their conservativeness and their shutting out of the world of the street, the Italians brought a memory of their café culture into restaurants which were bright and open, with big windows and bright colours. They leapt with enthusiasm on new materials and design trends that were coincidentally reactions to the same circumstances. Dark colours were replaced by light, bright surfaces, blackened timber floors and panels by mosaic, lino and vinyl. Heavy furniture was replaced by light, spindly designs, dim gaslights by glaring neons and funky shades.

The aesthetic was an eclectic blend of Americana, contemporary British and Italian details, pastel and bright colours, new artificial materials and little touches of Italy (cannelloni, Canalettos, gleaming frothy coffee machines, faded Juventus and Rocky Graziano posters).

And then there was the food. Some restaurateurs attempted to import Italian dishes but most abandoned them in the face of extreme English prejudice, although the ubiquitous spag bol remains a staple. Rather than repeat the boiled meat, boiled potatoes and boiled veg in a brown goo which formed the staple diet of the nation, the Italians chose a cunning blend of existing favourites (adding a few staples like roast beef and lamb): a mongrel menu born of fish and chips, breakfast, puddings and sandwiches. They took the best, easiest bits and created a national diet that can still be seen wherever the working classes travel en masse, from Torremolinos to Turkey.

TEA AND COFFEE

The history of the London café begins in Restoration London when traders from Venice and the Levant brought in coffee. The first coffee house was opened in Oxford in 1650, with the first in London two years later, by Pasqua Rosée, a former servant from Smyrna in Turkey. Within a few years the City was stuffed with smoky dens. They quickly became venues for business and dealing, particularly in the burgeoning insurance business. Edward Lloyd's coffee house, for instance, gave birth to the best-known name in insurance.

These early coffee houses were places to read the new newspapers, to conduct business, to politic, to gossip. They were male preserves and the

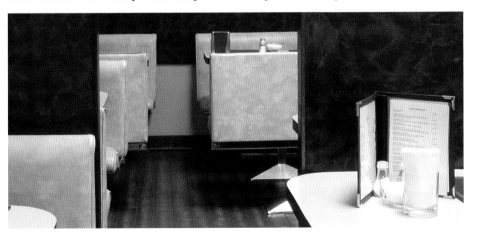

relative cheapness of the coffee or chocolate ensured that they did not become exclusive. They flourished in the City, around the Strand and in Covent Garden and became the centres of a new type of public and political debate. In the 18th century, the gentlemen's clubs began to take over this role as the forum, and the influence and number of coffee houses waned. However, reductions in the duty on imports during the 19th century made coffee an attractive drink for the working classes and a new breed of coffee rooms, simpler, starker and coarser versions of the old coffee houses, began to appear across the city. These coffee rooms played an important part in the education of the working classes, providing them with journals and newspapers, and also in weaning some away from alcohol. Whilst the pubs remained the default venues of the evening, coffee rooms, which served cheap meals or just bread and butter with coffee, began to dominate the early mornings. The caff culture of the workers' English breakfast began to take root in this era. These coffee rooms also became the favoured haunts of the city's radicals, the venue for the discussions and debates of an emerging left wing with Clerkenwell, Soho, Finsbury and Spitalfields being key nodes of the new culture.

The growing temperance movement also contributed to the rise of tea and coffee as an alternative to booze. The aim was to provide working men with an alternative to pubs and furnish them with nourishing food, newspapers and civilised discussion. Later in the century, the large coffee shop chains began to emerge, notably the ABC chain (oddly, the Aerated Bread Company) and J Lyons & Co, whose corner houses became the archetypal anonymous, big urban caffs. Over 100 opened in London alone and they dominated the cityscape until their demise in the 1970s. The milk bars that began to appear in the 1930s introduced slick Art Deco simplicity, usually featuring black and white tiling and polished chrome fittings. Their influence can still be detected in a few of the city's surviving caffs.

The big chains targeted a new market, the office worker. Furthermore, they appealed to both male and female workers: women could go for lunch or tea on their own in a manner which would have been unthinkable before the turn of the century. The same audience was the target for the sandwich bars that began to appear from the 1920s, one of the few types of catering in which London did lead the world.

HIP CAFFS & GREASY SPOONS

The 1950s brought a fundamental change with the optimism of a post-war generation and the influx of Italian immigrants who contributed a new culture of service and style. The genesis of the classic London caff coincided with, and is inseparable from, the growth of the coffee-bar culture during the 1950s.

The glamour of the new coffee bars must have been a shot of straight espresso into London's stewed-tea-filled veins. The Moka Bar in Soho's Frith Street was opened in 1953 by Gina Lollobrigida. The Moka was the first café in London to have a Gaggia coffee machine, the gleaming, spluttering beast that sat on the bar of all the hippest cafés and that introduced espresso and cappuccino into the language and the culture. In fact, the interior was designed around the espresso machine by architect Geoffrey Crockett and designer Maurice Ross for Pino Riservato, an Italian living in England whose disgust at the quality of British coffee prompted him to import the new Gaggia machines. The café was intended to illustrate the qualities of the coffee machine, a 3-D ad. The machines themselves were glorious creations of Italy's product-design culture, which also generated classics like the Vespa and Lambretta scooters – themselves closely related in their streamlined form to the coffee machines that created a steaming, throbbing heart in café interiors, a kind of regulator.

The Moka flourished partly due to the grateful local Italians of Soho, partly because of the young bohemian crowd it attracted. Its Gaggia and Formica interior became a template for the new London café and Soho became the heart of a new style. It is a cliché that British pop music was born in the espresso bars of Soho, but nevertheless it is true. As the centre of the music-publishing and film industries, as well as the heart of theatreland, Soho was as boho as you could go. A glimpse of the era can be had at the Bar Italia in

Frith Street, a London institution that for decades sold the only really fine coffee in the city. In the interior language of Bar Italia you can see what café owners across the city were trying to do and, whilst our book concentrates on the everyday, you can imagine the difference between the brightly lit, streamlined, lively space and the surrounding traditional restaurants and teashops. That Bar Italia has remained hip and lively also allows the visitor a tantalising glimpse of what that era must have meant for Soho.

But while the espresso bar may have played a pivotal role in British pop culture and swingingness, it shared only elements of interior décor with the traditional caff. These were throbbing, night-time places, media hubs, while the caff was resolutely daytime, only catering to clubbers who may have strayed out in the wee small hours (as the workers' caffs still do in Smithfield where meat porters share

booths with self-proclaimed creatives).

The first real blow for the workers' caff came with the arrival of fast food. Wimpy (part of the Lyons empire) opened its first place in 1953 while later chains including Chips with Everything, The Golden Egg and even the now ubiquitous Pizza Express brought sophisticated Pop Art graphics and design to the high street. In their wake came the big USA franchises KFC, McDonald's and Burger King, and it is these which have subsequently become the default choice of the working classes, leaving the few surviving caffs in an extremely vulnerable position. The fast-food joints brought American notions of universal design codes, classlessness and cleanliness, smiley if impersonal service, internationally consistent menus and limited but consistent choice – a McDonald's in north London is very little different from one in Nebraska. They add nothing to streetscape or local culture yet,

whether through marketing or taste, they have succeeded in conquering a couple of generations.

Fast food has irretrievably damaged caff culture – itself an earlier answer to the same need. But other trends also have dealt severe blows. During the 1970s and 1980s the high streets were deluged with kebab shops, usually run by Greeks and Turks, which seized an opportunity that the caffs failed to: opening at night. Catering to drunks and other victims of Britain's inexplicable licensing laws, they made themselves the default choice for chips, knocking out the traditional chippies even during the day. Chinese takeaways and curry houses did not dent the popularity or oeuvre of the caffs as they catered for the nocturnal population, although recently an interesting development has been the takeover of small caffs by Chinese or Thai caterers. In these the English menu and décor tend to remain whilst being supplemented with noodles and sweet & sour. It is a healthy compromise spoiling neither tradition and adding to the caff what spaghetti and lasagne must have done early in the last century.

The sandwich chains, however, are inflicting damage, particularly as more people now work in offices and tend to eat at their desks. The huge proliferation of coffee and sandwich bars in prominent high street locations has begun to supplant the caffs as the default lunch venue for office workers, although the caffs retain their more resolutely working class, usually male customers. Indeed, it is partly the image of healthy sandwiches and lady-friendly, American sitcom sofas that continues to attract females and young urban types to the chains.

The future of the caff remains profoundly insecure. Just during the writing of this book, perhaps a third of the places on my list have disappeared.

In other countries institutions like these, the last few remnants of a genuinely local urban culture, would be patronised, revered, perhaps protected. Here they remain in danger. The London caff has little, or none, of the glamour of an American diner, a French brasserie or an Italian, Spanish or Portuguese café with big metal and marble counters and white-shirted, bow-tied serving staff. Its interest is entirely of another kind, in the architecture of the everyday. London's old caffs act almost as found objects, *objets trouvé*. Their survival, with the functional anti-aesthetic of their interiors, is an antidote to the over-designed corporate chains that fill and suffocate our streets. They recognise the mundane, the ordinary and the importance of the local in our streetscape, and they satisfy a need for permanence and lack of change, anchors them into the community and the urban fabric. Their interior

aesthetic has become DIY, a series of stuck-on posters, special offers, dishes of the day and taped-up, failing components and Formica surfaces. Like Britain's railways, it is as if these interiors were constructed by a civilised race who have long departed and we can only tinker with the edges, having lost all the necessary technical and aesthetic skills. It is what must have happened when the Romans left their urban framework in the hands of the tribes of Britain who let it decay.

There is no way of reproducing the caffs. They are a physical manifestation of an era. It is not enough to buy a few kitchen chairs and scruffy tables and re-create an East End menu; the inevitable self-consciousness of any such effort renders it immediately unsuccessful. That is why it is so important not to lose these places, and to frequent them while we can.

Most of the literature about space, about architecture, design, interiors, bars and cafés concentrates on the extraordinary, the beautiful and the special. In the caffs we can see the remnants of a coherent vocabulary of the everyday, what Georges Perec has termed the infra-ordinary. It is to this notion that this guide is dedicated – to the idea that a flavour of an ordinary, everyday, but fast disappearing London can be sensed in these places. Caffs remain as outposts of the unmodernised, the undesigned; the last vestiges of the family business in a swamp of corporate conformity which has homogenised our streets so that they have become the blandest and ugliest of any European capital. Their tenacity is both a surprise and a testament to their necessity. Our streets and our city need the caffs more than they ever have.

SOHO

Gina Lollobrigida opening the Moka Bar at 29 Frith Street in Soho in 1953 seems as far away from our world of smoky, greasy caffs as it is possible to get. And it is. Soho, London's most clearly defined quarter, is hip, bohemian and cosmopolitan, and has been for at least a century. The collective arse of theatreland and the well-heeled West End and Mayfair, Soho's tight grid of streets succeeded Clerkenwell and Farringdon as the city's Little Italy at the end of the Second World War, and became home to a large Italian population. As the cool of Italian fashion, scooters, coffee and food began to usurp the now seemingly stuffy position of French *haute couture* and cuisine for a younger generation (and Soho used to be London's French quarter), the Italian immigrants established the beating heart of Soho in coffee bars which sprang up in the 1950s. In some ways, those Italian cafés are everything that our greasy spoons are not. Yet the gene pool is the same; the material vocabulary, the design intent, the urban presence, is shared. And that is why any examination of London's caffs would be incomplete without a look at Soho, but also why the quarter needs a section of its own. This is a world apart, not quite the realm of net curtains and greasy gingham which is being celebrated, or mourned, here.

Soho's coffee bars have been as important to its unique culture as its seedy drinking dens and sex shops, but their influence is waning, although you'd never think it to look at the place where any tour of Soho's coffee bars is doomed to start: the Bar Italia, a couple of doors down from the site of the Moka Bar on Frith Street. The Bar Italia is a throbbing slice of Italian pace, professionalism and sexiness. Almost uniquely in London, this place operates as a little piece of Italy, its white-shirted *baristas* are the real thing,

milking tarry espresso (still the best coffee in the city) out of the coffee machines. The Bar Italia, with its pictures (and the original gloves) of Rocky Graziano, its Formica counters, 1950s stools, acres of mirrors and bright fluorescents, is a kind of Ur caff, the Platonic ideal after which all others can only be a faint simulacrum. Vibrant and steaming, it has always been the *de rigueur* late-night destination for those in the know. Its nemesis is at the other end of Soho: the Centrale, a café so dingy and depressing that it almost made me want to abandon writing this book at all. The darkness of the Centrale, the naked light bulbs, the dark booths and scuzzy floors, as well as its proximity to dodgy cab-stands and open doors leading to the euphemistic models, help it leak a kind of existential angst, a dark, brooding horror. Definitely not Festival of Britain and it's easy to see why it was a favourite of nihilist punks and self-pitying resting actors.

Then there's Old Compton Street, formerly the main drag of Little Italy, more recently the venue for London's gay *passeggiata*. The continental patisseries survive, the original Valerie's retains the bohemian European feel instituted by its Belgian founder in the 1920s. This is the home of the student staples: the Pollo Bar and the Stockpot. The latter is part of a useful little chain of bohemian restaurants, not quite caffs but serving lasagne with chips and carrots, and cheap puddings with custard, in a traditional, and extremely cheap, vein. The Pollo however is a triumph of 1960s Pop design, a reminder of a time when Soho was cool. The gorgonzola, cheesy decoration of the Amalfi further down the street shows that not everything the Italians did was cool, reinforced by the Alpine-chalet chic of the Lorelei in nearby Bateman Street. The 101 Snack Bar on Charing Cross Road has had its name neutered to the generic Snack Bar. Yet its brilliantly lit, bright yellow and black striated interior, the counter, its attendant stools and terrazzo floor, still give an idea of how much of a beacon these coffee bars must have been in the dreary 1950s cityscape. It still looks striking. Similarly the bright orange sign of Zita (just outside Soho at the northern end of Shaftesbury Avenue) gives off a whiff of 1950s jazz.

The corporatisation of Soho has been widely reported and studied, and the chains are steaming into its tight grid of streets. Yet the resilience of the sex industry, the rag trade and scuzzy music shops seems almost infinite and Soho's caffs are surviving better than caffs are elsewhere. Perhaps this is partly because of a more developed sense of irony, and partly because they have become institutions and the sheer footfall allows them to carry on as they are. Maybe it is also due to the comparatively strong residential presence and the predominance of bohemian trades from the theatrical and literary to graphics and film, which all appreciate the ambience and continuity that they provide. The Soho caffs remain a kind of distinctive sub-genre, just as Soho remains a little (and shrinking) slice of bohemia. It retains strong traces of its cosmopolitan history and its cafés too remain separate: less working class, often licensed, usually with late opening – many of the things which, in my extraordinarily strict taxonomy, disqualify them from inclusion in the gazetteer. As a dense, walkable, potted history of the evolution of the caff, however, the streets of Soho remain unbeatable.

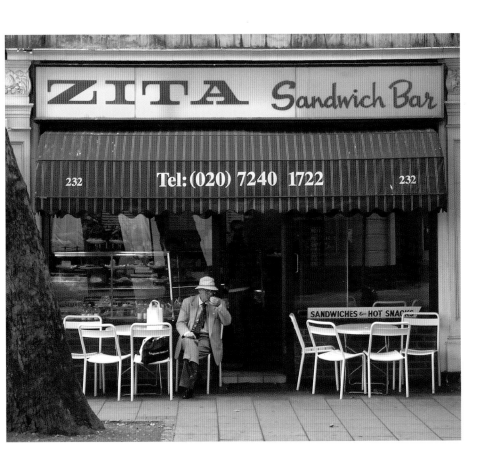

WEST LONDON
HALF MOON CAFE

125 FULHAM PALACE ROAD W6
TUBE: HAMMERSMITH

Part of an ensemble of shops that seem to have been left behind, the Half Moon is a thrilling survival. Tiny and almost invisible, I must have walked past it dozens of times before I noticed it. The most striking thing is the surviving white Vitrolite ceiling, an elaborate construction accommodating all the ceiling joists, which is very similar to the one in the River Cafe. The counter is a blend of black Vitrolite and frosted glass, a lovely glimmer of Deco glamour. Most of the walls also retain their original pink and light-green marbled panelling (with black string-courses) plastic fantastic. Repairs have been done in a crudely delightful manner – getting by and making do.

The story here is in the details: the evocatively worn threshold, the cracked but intact terrazzo floor, the almost Art Nouveau door handle stuck onto a reinforcing plate, the cabinet of curiosities which stands next to the window, the faded, almost illegible plastic Pepsi sign above the door.

The brown-painted woodwork betrays another England. The clash between wartime austerity and brown-sauce decorating and the Moderne world of Art Deco artificial materials is made manifest in a slightly schizophrenic scheme, compounded by folksy trattoria furniture. It is noticeable quite how much the wrong type of furniture detracts from the caff feel.

The whole atmosphere, from the green, original frontage to the eclectic, scratched and patched interior, evokes the cosy world of a local bar in a grey, industrial town in Belgium or northern France, a kind of bleak Maigret world.

Do not miss the other dinosaurs around here: Kay's florist next door and, especially, the I Mark (Modern Footwear) shoe store with a shop display which seems about ready for rationing and bomb tape on the windows. It seems the incessant traffic has made this bit of road so unattractive to developers that they've left it alone. Good.

PETERBOROUGH CAFE

Incongruously placed in posh Parson's Green, the Peterborough Cafe seems to be the last bastion of proletarian culture left here. It is hard to imagine two worlds further apart than the clientele of the Sloaney Pony on the other side of the green and the consumers of the Full English at this little shack of a caff.

The canted Formica counter sits on a raised dais on a murky blue lino floor. Apart from this, the caff is notable for its almost complete lack of colour. It is as if it had seeped into the ground, or perhaps into the frying oil. Even the old boxing posters on the walls fail to inject any life. However, the enormous handwritten menu scrawled over almost an entire wall is an achievement, a kind of Rosetta stone of caff culture waiting to communicate its language of the endless repetition of sausages, bacon, eggs and beans in seemingly infinite combinations.

There are some archaeologically interesting signs on one wall including the enigmatic 'Tea 'n' coffee' (late 1970s?), 'We serve hot pies (extra steam)' and 'A Tasty Snack - Toasted Sandwiches'. The glass counter-top vitrine is adorned with perhaps the least appetising illustration of a sandwich I have yet seen. The basic, wooden furniture is solid and sensible – chairs and stools which have survived well – but there's no funky Formica here, just utilitarian surfaces. Net curtains on the outside, and another to the kitchen, and simple timber-boarded walls complete the effect. A good red cafe sign announces its presence towards the New Kings Road.

That this is the English (rather than the Italian) end of caff catering is visible in every facet of the operation, from the complete lack of aesthetic intention to the grim service. Yet, perhaps because of this relentless functionalism, there is a certain charm here.

P GEORGE SNACK BAR

There's something almost Parisian about the little courtyard on the corner of which stands P George's. The Edwardian mansion block comes from a different world from the caff, yet they've grown together, while all the other shops seem to change annually.

P George's is a bit of a star, having appeared alongside Terence Stamp in Ken Loach's 1967 film of Nell Dunn's *Poor Cow*. In our parallel universe it retains a touch of star quality, its big, wide windows announcing it to the world – no need for net curtains or blinds here. This does mean, though, that there is no intimacy at all. The interior is cold, the furniture (a curious-looking bench and table, perhaps knocked-off picnic sets from Slovakia) hard and the clientele pretty miserable. Otherwise, the traditional elements are all here: coffee machine with a priapic, distended flue, tongue-and-groove-clad walls and exterior, grim fluorescent tubes, good old enthusiastically misspelt menus and nice old coke decals in the window. This does seem a genuine refuge for the dispossessed, its solitary atmosphere leavened only by a few posties from next door. The cafe remains the antidote to Swinging London.

RIVER CAFE

The caff closest to my office and to my heart, the River Cafe, is one of the finest and most intact survivals from a golden age of dining rooms. The wonderful details stretch back to the interwar era. Indeed, the blue decorative wall tiles represent the last gasp of Art Nouveau influence while the lotus leaf capitals on the cast-iron columns hint at the transition to Art Deco and the discovery of Tutankhamen's tomb in the 1920s. The intact Vitrolite ceiling floats high over a generous space with none of the stuffy cosiness of the genre. The mosaic floor, however, is from a later era, as is the sturdy kitchen furniture and the aluminium ashtrays.

Some of the highlights are the Italian posters on the walls (one brutally cut off by the underside of the stairs). Years of exposure to smoke, fried bacon and chips have left them with the deep-brown patina of old masters. The old lettering survives, advertising services such as Coffee, Breakfast [Light Refreshments] etc. above a deep-green, glazed brick plinth.

The long counter is a little worse for wear and is due to be replaced. The Italian football posters on the wall behind, however, seem here to stay, along with the chianti bottles and ceramic pots which were once *de rigueur* shorthand for Italian food. The River Cafe is undoubtedly one of the best, if not the best, surviving cafe in London. Only L Rodi's can come close but it lacks the coherence of its Fulham contemporary. The space remains generous and largely unaltered.

There is also an endless patience in the way the staff here answer the phone and field enquiries for the other River Cafe, the one in Hammersmith run by Ruth Rogers and Rose Gray. They're both Italian but you get the impression that the sprinkling of celebs and New Labour types would get distinctly (and utterly unjustifiably) apoplectic if they ended up here.

WEST END & CENTRAL
BLOOMSBURY RESTAURANT

It is peculiarly English that the caff at the heart of London's most futuristic, monumental and monolithic piece of urbanism should be a quaint, dated little number with gingham curtains and a supremely naff mural of swans. In a heroic piece of 1960s concrete modernism (inspired by the visionary drawings of Italian Futurism) the Bloomsbury's walls are clad in fake-brick wallpaper. The modernism must have seemed too much.

Nevertheless, from the cool, original, metal-framed window it's obvious that this clash of styles must be worth a second look. The seating, clad in studded slime-green Leatherette, is comfortable and hideous. The colour is provided by the swans and by a series of Day-Glo star stickers and assorted odd plastic signs introduced to the walls in some word association game – 'cappuccino', for instance, just sits there, on its own. It's a bit like the way older caffs used to have signs exhorting you to drink 'Nice Fresh Milk'.

Considering its location (both geographically and architecturally) there is something strangely provincial about the Bloomsbury. It can never have fitted in. It also manages to skilfully avoid any of the elegance of the 1960s design that surrounds it.

DA GIOVANNI

Not your ordinary caff, this. From the geometric reliefs on the ceramic door handles to the kitsch, stagy paintings in niches, this is the art end of the cafforama. Da Giovanni's fizzes with a remarkable energy and is a curious result of Italians seemingly aiming at the local Jewish market – all salt beef and pastrami. Its cosmopolitan buzz gives it a whiff of a fast, brash, New York lunch counter.

The creamy ceramic door handles match the tiles both outside and behind the counter – relics from a pop age when Marylebone was hip as hell and even the Beatles had their HQ down the road. The celebs hanging on the wall testify. Good little pendant lights with chunky, caricatured bulbs hang over the tables from fake beamed ceilings; dark wood lines the walls; the floors are in appropriate and worn salmon and cream-cheese terrazzo. The furniture, with the exception of a booth by the window, is dull. It is nevertheless a fantastic, atmospheric interior with a phenomenal buzz, and one of the city's more sophisticated caffs.

Right opposite lurks the Hellenic, a slice of old London catering stuck in aspic, all net curtains and rustic plastering. Nearby also is the Marylebone at 58 Marylebone Lane, a good surviving example of the caff; and just up the lane at 35 is Paul Rothe, a surviving old school deli and sandwich counter. This is what English catering must have looked like before the Italians got to it. Nice, definitely worth having a look at, but a bit Trumpton.

EURO SANDWICH BAR

20 SWALLOW STREET W1B
TUBE: PICCADILLY CIRCUS

A tiny pimple on the backside of the gloriously overscaled arse of Regent Street, the Euro Snack Bar keeps company with London's oldest curry house and a bunch of seedy clubs; on a street which once linked Piccadilly with Oxford Street but seems to have little purpose except to give buildings a back. The blue swallow on the big orange sign tells you which street you're in, and probably what decade. Inside, the caff is tiny and cosy with tight booths and an extremely low ceiling. Plastic plants dangle from a high shelf in a pale imitation of life while the carefully framed pictures on the wall attempt to make art of baked potato with baked beans, baked potato with butter, bacon and chips; and so on.

For someone who usually uses photos of food as an excuse to leave, I found the framing method rather charming.

The Leatherette seats are comfortable and the subtle curves on the edges of the tables sophisticated, but best of all are the little shelves for the green, Deco-ish sugar-bowls (offering white and brown) and cruets. They are placed like a sacral offering or holy water – a kind of salt and pepper stoup. Everything is covered in real or fake wood: the walls are the woodiest of almost any London caff. It seems to have survived because, like the Brook's Mews Sandwich Bar, no one except the steady stream of regulars knows it's there.

EURO
SANDWICH BA
BREAKFAST NO:1 BACON
SAUSAGE , EGG,TOMATOES,
BEANS, CHIPS, 2 TOAST
TEA OR COFFEE
BREAKFAST NO:2 BACON,
2 EGGS, CHIPS BEANS,2TOA T
TEA OR COFFEE
SANDWICHES, BAPS,
AGUETTES, ROLLS, SALADS,
AKED POTATOES, PIES, CHIPS,
COFFEE, TEA, CAPPUCINO,
COLD DRINKS SWEETS,
CIGARETTES,ICE CREAM

JOHN'S SANDWICH BAR

36A BERNERS STREET W1T
TUBE: OXFORD CIRCUS

Small, cramped and great. There's a big, unusually appetising sandwich counter, crappy pics of Formula 1 cars on the walls and an unusual counter front featuring an abstract, metallic relief. Terracotta Leatherette seats, brown kitchen flooring, brown Formica table tops, timber-clad walls, Fresh Milk sticker on the fridge, great old coffee machine – the bits are all here. This is a rare refuge for workers who seem to devour the food with the knowledge that it's on its way out.

At the other end of the street, number 80 is Avella's, another good, though slightly pricier caff catering more to the office crowds.

LINO'S CAFÉ

This used to be Sidoli's Buttery, owned by a family who were among the kings of the caff world. It's been partly updated but retains a good 1970s feel with bright yellow tiles behind the counter and outside, green Leatherette banquettes and timber tongue-and-groove panelled walls. What must be the biggest menu in London can be seen over the counter – plus photos, which almost disqualified it as I can't stand photos of food.

The big squares on the chequerboard terrazzo floor are worn in a way which suggest as they might be older than the décor, so does the odd red-painted ceiling with all the original mouldings.

SANDWICH BAR

The last caff in Mayfair is at the arse end of Claridge's. The two worlds could hardly be more different, yet both are survivals from an earlier, more stratified London, a city where class was built into the urban fabric; the mews for the proles and servants, Brook Street for the toffs. This is resolutely not a back entrance to Gordon Ramsay's.

As simple and straightforward as its name, Sandwich Bar is a prime piece of utility caff. From the 1960s font of the fascia to the menu in the window, this is as authentic as it gets. The interior has been drained of any colour except slime green and knackered wood, the fluorescents sucking any last vestiges of colour out of even the sauce bottles. The beautifully preserved trad, double-barrelled coffee machine splutters away on a bland Formica counter, the washed-out finish of which is echoed throughout the serving area. The furniture includes, unusually for London, Thonet bentwood-style chairs, the classic central European café design, as well as comfy Leatherette-clad utility versions. The tables, however, are standard Formica-topped kitchen style. The usual motifs are all here, lots of wood effect, net curtains, disparate pictures. You can tell it's Mayfair – they have fruit on the counter.

MAMA'S

A tiny, tidy and rather poignant south London caff, Mama's is utterly representative of the plain little eateries which form the backbone of this collection. But it is surprising to see it here at the heart of London's cultural complex.

Tongue-and-groove boarded walls reach up to dado level and the occasional pot plant does little to brighten up the interior. In fact, only the vernacular plastic ketchup bottles succeed in bringing any colour to the interior at all. But there is one extraordinary and notable feature: the furniture looks like something you'd see at the Milan Fair at the time of writing. The fixed, grey seating is austere and elegant, the slope on the backs just right, the white of the tables matches it perfectly and the spindly fixed legs are as hip as could be. Stealth minimalism.

Otherwise Mama's is exactly what you'd expect from the outside, a hole-in-the-wall serving counter at the rear, nasty tiles, a good, frothing coffee machine and Day-Glo cut-out signs in the window. I don't think I've seen a more poignant image of English streetscape than Sue's shot through these signs to the OAP at the bus stop. Heartbreaking.

METROPOLITAN CAFE

The tacky green powder-coated fascia of the Metropolitan offers not a hint of the sumptuous interior. Yet the Deco tinged bar and the terrific back wall announce one of London's most atmospheric interiors.

The Metropolitan was owned by the same clan as the Regent Milk Bar just down the road which was, until recently, the finest example of the diner-influenced pastel ice-cream parlour to have survived. Its demise makes the tenacity of the much smaller Metropolitan all the more special. The canted counter is made up of panels of mint green, cream and black, kind of Moderne Mondrian. The shiny coffee machine sits modestly to one side allowing the flash illuminated late Deco panel on the back wall to shine (Good Food—Good Taste). The opposite wall is adorned with stepped mirrors framed in black and cream Vitrolite.

The furniture is from a different era altogether: solid and supremely comfortable mid-century chairs with curved ply backs, and monochrome Formica tables with 1960s squiggles. This is a rare taste of the jolly milk bar style, pastels and whiffs of Hollywood Deco with a complete absence of the existential angst and emptiness of the classic London caff. For that go around the corner to the pinks walls and wood effect of Mario & Mike's at 125 Boscombe Street. Authentically grim.

The high-security Paddington Green police station is opposite, where top terrorists are held, and it seems to be the coppers in plain or not so plain clothes who keep the Metropolitan going strong. Its depressing grey mass can be glimpsed beyond the extraordinary leaning towers of cones in the window.

THE NEW PICCADILLY

8 DENMAN STREET W1D
TUBE: PICCADILLY CIRCUS

This caff is the business. All the furniture and fittings have, incredibly, survived intact, but there is a self-consciousness here which lifts the New Piccadilly slightly outside the typology defined in this book. The menu even appeals to customers to 'Enjoy our 1950s menu and café'. The waiters, dressed up somewhere between mental hospital orderlies and sailors, may look a little ropey but the space itself is the real thing. From the terrific signage outside to the Cadillac pink customised coffee machine, this amazing, intact survival is both a missing link between the slightly showbiz, slightly sleazy world of 1950s Soho and the working-class genesis of the Formica caff.

The waisted, red wall-mounted light fittings supply an instant Festival of Britain vibe complementing the red vinyl booths. The horse-shoe-shaped hanging menu embraces a very cool contemporary plastic clock, while a sequence of truly odd pediments crowns the fluorescents above the counter. At the rear bits of dark-stained tongue-and-groove panelling and Thonet chairs and coat stands combined with theatre and art posters, begin to evoke a local Parisian café. There has always been something continental about Soho, the result of its blend of inhabitants from French through to Italian. The good patisseries of Old Compton Street testify eloquently to its history.

PERDONI'S

18–20 KENNINGTON ROAD SE1
TUBE: KENNINGTON

Big by caff standards, Perdoni's with its swish cream-coloured Leatherette booth seating has something of the feel of a US coffee lounge or urban diner. From a later period than the standard London caff, Perdoni's doesn't display the usual stylistic traits. Nevertheless, it is a coherent and unified design which fits into its double street-frontage comfortably. Like so many London institutions, Perdoni's is big on brown. From the perfunctory sign outside (repeated on the vinyl menus) to the floor, tables, blotchy beige tiles and coppery tones of the walls and fittings, this is a late-terracotta caff.

Big, spacious and busy, Perdoni's is a blend of tough, hard-wearing urbanity and kitsch. By the time it was fitted out (late 1970s/early 1980s) caffs were no longer bringing modernism to the urban working classes. They had lapsed into a twee, suburban genre far less strident than the fake rural idyll of the big pubs, but retrograde nevertheless. This is ironic given Perdoni's harsh setting: the relentlessly grim estates of a south London which never recovered from the war. It is here because of its size, feel and terrific steel and vinyl flip-up furniture, not because of its style.

PIMLICO
REGENCY CAFE

Pimlico is an extraordinary mix of posh and prole. Its backstreets seem stuck in a post-war warp, with fragments of a London long gone elsewhere surviving here. One such is the Regency Cafe, an authentic slice of late Deco London. The black-tiled exterior and the stark modernist typeface of the sign give way to a stripped utilitarianism that has echoes of Deco, but only faintly audible ones. The sign above the door says established 1946 and the cream tiles of the interior, broken up by slim, black string-courses, attest to that date. The seating is less authentic. Brown moulded seats and fixed tables point to a 1970s refit while the green tongue-and-groove boarding around the counter looks a bit too clean and tasteful. However, a number of superb fittings have survived. Look out for the old, black, contemporary coat-hooks with coloured baubles, as well as a railway clock and an assortment of old adverts and posters including a great 1960s example ('Stop for coffee — it's delicious') and some anachronistic coke ads.

The utilitarian localness of the place has the faintest hint of working-class Paris. Maybe it's the red gingham curtains preserving the diners' privacy; maybe it's the late, stripped Deco-style which was so predominant in France. It has meant that the café has been used extensively in film and TV productions, so it may feel strangely familiar.

The Regency is in the middle of one of London's mini Deco zones, which is worth strolling around. Almost next door, in Page Street is Lutyens' 1928 chequerboard social housing scheme, the 1929 Horticultural Hall is a street away and, in a tiny Moderne corner building on Regency Place and Maunsell Street, is the Astral Cafe, another working man's survivor now kept going by Westminster cabbies.

THE WILTON SNACK BAR

78 WILTON ROAD SW1V
TUBE: VICTORIA

Another Pimlico curio, the Wilton is a
1960s caff with most of its bits still
intact. The big orange letters of the
sign announce that this is one of the
few cafes in the area not to have been
modernised or taken over by a chain.

From the orange pendant globe
lights in the window to the slender blue
mosaic-tiled columns, from the terrazzo
tiled floors to the brown Leatherette
and timber banquettes, it all seems
to have survived. The classic stick-on-
letter menu faces the street from inside,
and the fragment of red and grey
wallpaper behind the counter is almost
worth listing on its own. There's also a
sign, 'The management cannot accept
responsibility for hats, coats, umbrellas
etc', which comes straight out of the
traditional English non-service culture.
Not special but good. Lippy staff, too.

ISLINGTON ALPINO

The elegant, sparse sign and dark wood fascia combined with the Islington setting could lead you to believe that this is another overpriced eatery. Far from it. Peer in through the windows at the neat rows of fixed seating, the dark wood pilasters and the wood-clad counter and you'll see a cool, elegant, coherent, late Art Deco interior.

Some of the old, late modernist light fittings have survived as real museum pieces and, as a typical example of caffism, the old modernist lights that didn't survive were replaced by new traditional kitsch. The salmon-pink walls and fluted pilasters would look at home in a slightly seedy 1930s hotel, but the furniture – solid wood and Leatherette seating and chunky Formica-topped tables with rounded corners – is the genuine item.

Just down the road Manze's Eel and Pie shop, a branch of London's most famous eel chain, is a superb example of a peculiarly London style, a kind of ecclesiastical municipal with its blend of acres of tiles leavened with Arts and Crafts details and delicately turned, but solid, high-backed booths.

The caff version of *Invasion of the Body Snatchers*, the lights are on but there's nobody home. On one level we should be grateful that this gem of an Art Deco café has survived in an area where few restaurants last more than a few years. On the other hand, it is also a demonstration of how easy it is to rip the heart out of a caff without altering the physical fabric in any way, an example of exactly how fragile the caff can be.

The original details have been retained but the menu, and subsequently the clientele, have changed. S & M (Sausage and Mash, and formerly the much more caff-ish Alfredo's) has become a licensed restaurant, with a wine list and a few caff staples coexisting awkwardly with posher nosh and prices to match. The formerly working-class customers have been replaced by an eccentric mishmash of antiques traders, trendies and celebs. The atmosphere of the original has disappeared, showing how class-based London's caff culture remains.

Nevertheless, the preservation of such a cornucopia of original features is a blessing. From the mosaic threshold (Refreshments) to the original signage (Ices 3d.4d.6d/Teas etc.), every detail is fine. The chromed frontage and big windows evoke an American diner – so obviously the counterpart of London's caffs yet so radically different.

CLERKENWELL & CITY
ANDREWS

160 GRAY'S INN ROAD WC1X
TUBE: CHANCERY LANE/KING'S CROSS ST PANCRAS

A big, well-preserved original, Andrews is often peppered with celebrities and media types yet retains its character as a real working-class haven. The mix of suits, Prada and high-visibility vests is testament to the enduring, cross-class appeal of the old-style, no-style caff with its Full English and chips with everything offer.

The big, surprisingly condensation-free windows advertise Teas & Snacks in the original lettering between the vent-axias, and the old coffee machine splutters and gurgles at the centre of the counter. The look is stripped-down, archetypal caff with tongue-and-groove panelling up to the dado, the wall acting as the usual makeshift photo gallery – good flamenco dancer, nice gondolas too.

The fittings are sparse: a couple of diagonally placed mirrors, contemporary zag-zig, baubled coat-hooks (very Festival of Britain) and a streamlined wall-heater. The furniture also is the real thing, solid Formica-topped tables and old kitchen chairs.

BARBICAN GRILL

A little remnant of knackered,
unreconstructed London in an area
which has been ravaged by
yuppification. The usual green
Leatherette banquettes are
here supplemented by hideous
domestic wallpaper. I like the
island banquette topped off with
a single chair which channels
traffic through the caff's two aisles,
a kind of nascent caff urbanism.
Good tiled floor, tongue-and-grooved
walls and a variegated ceiling.
Unspectacular but good; a rare
surviving local.

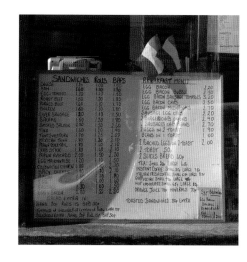

BEPPE'S

23 WEST SMITHFIELD EC1A
TUBE: FARRINGDON

Smithfield is Breakfast Inc. The carnivorous meat porters ensure that bacon, sausage and egg with all the trimmings is available any time of the day to suit their semi nocturnal hours. The area used to be teeming with caffs but they've thinned out a lot in recent years. Their absence is partly compensated for by the unusual opening hours of the pubs around here, a special dispensation to cater for the traders and porters, and the early morning trade.

Beppe's is a good, standard London caff. The green and brown glazed bricks on the facade piers give it a solid, slightly municipal, Edwardian feel. There's a fine protruding sign with a steaming cup of coffee and knife and fork for the less literate among us. Hot Snacks & Sandwich Bar it proclaims for the rest.

The boarded door displays a terrific 1960s pull handle in brass and wood and leads into a packed space stuffed with timber and Leatherette booths. Plastic plants and fruit hang from the walls but the interior highlight is the jazzy panels of pressed copper on both the counter front and the fascia above it, which I think are close cousins of the greyer version in John's in Mortimer Street. Good little cantilevered steel shelves offer up ketchup and condiments like a mini stoup.

Two naked light bulbs hang in the window illuminating the takeaway bags. Nice touch.

COPPER GRILL

25–27 ELDON STREET EC2M
TUBE: LIVERPOOL STREET

The wonderful fascia sign on the Copper Grill looks like something from a 1970s box of matches. The flaming pan and brilliant yellow ground could hardly make this curious survival stand out more. The bathroom tiles adorning the facade indicate that this could be a pure, unreconstructed gem, and so it proves.

The cafe may be teeming with objectionable City lads but the interior manages to compensate for the clientele with a wonderful blend of period features. The spread of black Leatherette-clad banquettes is impressive, and the huge plate-glass windows give extraordinary views onto the city, unusually unhindered by net curtains. The downstairs section is more utilitarian but the odd, DIY Deco serving counter is unique, like something built by a carpenter who was told about the interiors of Miami Modern hotels and decided to make something similar without ever having seen them. The weirdly upbeat murals evoke some early vision of Milton Keynes – very odd, but they do add some colour.

The Copper Grill may well be gone by the time of publication; the City will be a duller place without it.

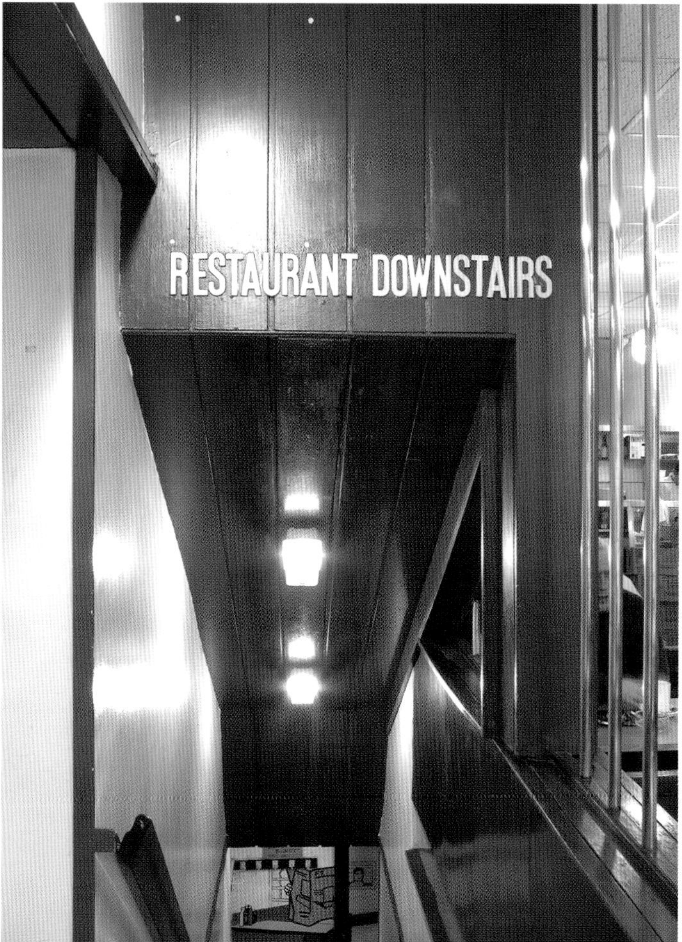
RESTAURANT DOWNSTAIRS

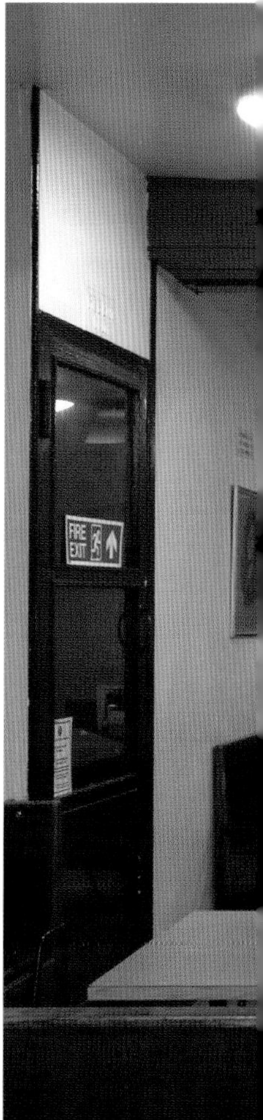
FIRE
EXIT

FARINA'S

61 LEATHER LANE EC1N
TUBE: CHANCERY LANE/FARRINGDON

This fine London greasy spoon is seasoned with a little Chinese in an unusual combination that seems to detract from neither oeuvre. The lucky, waving porcelain cats on the counter give the game away.

This is not a really old caff, but it retains a great atmosphere and is a survivor from the days when this was still the heart of Little Italy. The interior exhibits a very English, very limited colour scheme of turd browns and snot greens, roughly the constituents of a tweed jacket, but it's not unpleasant. In fact, the chunky, marbled, green Formica tables seem to shine in the gloom. The counter and walls are adorned with dull, dark timber and primitive appliqué mouldings but touches like the single, artistically positioned potted plant (in a pale pink vase) behind the spindly, iron stair-rails give the interior a forlorn eccentricity which makes it quite unique. The Leatherette booth seating is comfortable, the old coffee machine survives, the choice of food is impressive and the place is kept livelier than the dull interior would suggest by the market traders of Leather Lane.

Speial Vegelarian
Prawn Crackers Spring r
and vegetable fried Rice
£ 4.0

Special V

Spare Ribs wi
Rice Prawn Cra
Roll (2)

Beef or Chicken
with Prawn Cra
Roll (2)

Sweet Sour Ch
with Prawn Cra
Roll (2)

Value Meal
Curry Tomato, Chicken
Beef Curry with food
and Prawn Crackers
£ 4.50

GOLDEN FISH BAR

102 FARRINGDON ROAD EC1R
TUBE: FARRINGDON

A bit of a cuckoo here, the Golden Fish Bar has crept in against the odds. It is a fish and chip shop rather than a traditional caff, but it constitutes a survival of such purity that it is a kind of archetype and deserves its place. Unlike many of the caffs run by other Italians, there is not much clutter here. The fixed furniture, with its fake dark wood veneer, is staggeringly simple and surprisingly elegant with none of the kitchen clumsiness more often associated with these places. Just simple bent-tube frames and solid surfaces: remarkably contemporary. The space is hardly leavened by the dark timber panelling and monochrome floor. This is an austere interior with none of the pastel Formica fun or assorted kitsch that lightens other similar interiors. From the archaic-looking menus to the original crockery, this is a very fine caff indeed.

Just a couple of doors down at 92 is the Quality Chop House. Absolutely not a caff in that it is now posh and expensive, this is nevertheless an important and surprising survival, an original dining room crowded with high-backed, almost ecclesiastical booths. According to the original signage this is the home of 'London noted cup of tea', with 'Quick service' and 'Civility'. Unfortunately this is no longer where you will find 'Progressive working class catering' but it gives a fine idea of what it would have been like.

MURATORI

162 FARRINGDON ROAD EC1R
TUBE: FARRINGDON/KING'S CROSS ST PANCRAS

The brownest caff in London, Muratori is a rare survival from the pre-Formica days of London's caff culture. The timber-panelled exterior follows through to the interior where a couple of the original high-backed pews survive. The panelled walls are topped off by a collection of framed black-and-white photos and the whole is very visible from outside, the big windows unusually unhindered by net curtains or condensation. The counter area is a later refit, a beige and brown tiled mass – not nice.

The interior, which appears to have been coloured with the brown sauce on the tables, is stuffed with postal workers from Mount Pleasant, which possibly accounts for its rare survival.

MURATORI
CAFÉ
Heroes For Six Minutes 2
WHITE COLLAR BOXING
YORK HALL
VERTIGO
VERTIGO

PICCOLO BAR

21ELDON STREET EC2M
TUBE: LIVERPOOL STREET

A very odd little place, the Piccolo is a schizophrenic venue halfway between a local caff and a bohemian bistro. The tight, upstairs takeaway counter does a busy trade to City types, while the restaurant is downstairs, reached via a mean little stairway.

The fascia signage is amateurish and good; the word sandwich between 'Piccolo' and 'Bar' has been made into the sandwich filling. The Piccolo has something rather European about it, like a little backstreet café in Porto or Bilbao. A Victorian-style hand is meant to point to the 'Restaurant Downstairs' (behind) but in fact almost always points at black bags of rubbish (in front). This is unlikely to be an ironic joke.

There is something of the feel of a jazz club or some alternative 1950s slice of after-dark bohemia. The lurid blue and pink of the imitation-mosaic Formica table-tops, the Artex arches, the mix and mismatch plastic signs, the kitsch chalet light fittings – this is not a pretty (and certainly not a coherent) interior. But it is great fun and, given its central location, a good and pleasant surprise.

THE REGIS

In an extraordinary location on the edge of Horace Jones' fussy, Victorian Leadenhall Market (Jones was also the architect of Tower Bridge) and opposite Richard Rogers' clunking money-making machine of Lloyds Building, this tiny caff is another unexpected survival. Lloyds, of course, started off in one of the City's coffee houses, these being the default forums for 17th- and 18th-century discussion, gossip, politics, news and business. Now the City types, the brokers, dealers and bankers, are more likely to frequent the chains for overpriced and oversized coffees, but the Regis nevertheless does a steady trade.

There are no tables and chairs here, just a counter with fixed bar stools. The beamed ceiling is old and saggy, and supports a number of original glass globe pendants. The counter is centred on the usual frothy coffee machine. Otherwise, the dark panelled detailing is stolid and unspectacular. The outside sign, with its simple, stripped-down font, is very cool.

S & D
Rapacioli
Partnership
trading as
Regis Snack
Bar

ROSA'S CAFE

12 HANBURY STREET E1
TUBE: LIVERPOOL STREET/ALDGATE EAST

An odd little showbiz enclave, Rosa's is an aesthetic jumble with grey Formica-clad walls and tacky marbling, horrible pubby chairs (and a few solid catering staples), late 1970s tiles and messy handwritten notices all over the shop. One corner is reserved as a mini shrine to music-hall star Bud Flanagan (remembered here with his partner Chesney Allen) who lived above the shop. Another corner is dedicated to that other East End double act, Gilbert and George, who used to frequent the much-mourned Market Café.

Nice 1970s drop light fittings but little else of note. Rosa's is interesting more for its survival, and its position as the hip heart of the (increasingly bourgeois and wealthy) east London art scene, than anything else.

SCOTTI'S SNACK BAR

39 CLERKENWELL GREEN EC1R
TUBE: FARRINGDON

One of the few genuine working-men's caffs left in the heart of what used to be radical London. From Chartists to Marxists, Clerkenwell Green has seen the departure of more demos and riots than any other part of the city and its coffee rooms, venues for the disaffected and self-educated skilled workers who populated its suffocating slums, were pivotal in left-wing gatherings and debates.

Now the caffs have been displaced by gastro-pubs and coffee chains, and radical debate continues only at the Marx Memorial Library. Scotti's remains as a little taster of an earlier era. The route from front to back is clearly marked in its scuffed tile-floor, a path to tea and bacon rolls which are, extraordinarily, still fried on a gas cooker behind the red Formica-clad bar.

The monochrome black and white, squiggly check wall-covering is replaced above the dado by a dun domestic wallpaper which bubbles up in resentment at its own incongruity.

The dado itself serves as a makeshift picture rail for a gallery including a sketch of the caff and a photo of the Italian village whence came the Scottis. The pictures mingle with an extreme selection of proletarian kitsch which now looks quite avant-garde. The counter is dominated by the big, shiny urn flanked by two glass cases of sandwiches and cakes. The fittings, too, look the business, from the streamlined wall-heaters to the glass ceiling lights and the old, honey-pot-style door-closer to the excellent Formica-topped tables. The only thing that doesn't quite fit is the big, mirrored wall unit behind a counter that resembles something out of an apothecary, shop, but is stuffed with packs of coffee and Italian delicacies. Finally, don't miss the museum-piece ashtrays – old, metallic red and blue bits of pressed aluminium distributed free by cigarette companies, Parker and Senior Service. Like Scotti's itself, remarkable survivals.

THE SHEPHERDESS

Hoxton was a notorious, continuous slum. It is arguable that since its takeover by creatives it has become less attractive. Bits of its rougher past have survived. The Shepherdess is amongst the survivals to be grateful for. It has, remarkably, avoided creativisation. The resolutely unhip imitation bamboo, fixed metal seating (with yellow Leatherette) is powerfully ugly (although the banquettes around the perimeter are better). The check curtains badly painted on the windows do little to enhance the aesthetic. Yet the almost wholly unattractive interior retains the feel of a proper London caff.

The original shepherdess logo outside, a kind of Marie Antoinette playing at rural like the Hoxtonites playing at being a bit working class, is terrific, as is the whole sign. Huge windows give views onto the deeply unattractive surroundings and into the brilliantly lit and buzzy interior.

VERNASCA

Another market caff – the old-style
eateries survive better with a ready-
made, captive constituency. Vernasca
is another moment of deep-browndom,
a chocolate shell. It is also, as a result,
very cosy without the coldness that
often affects these places. Everything
that can be is wood-grained: table tops,
walls, seating, counter front... Apart
from this there is very little to point
out specifically; only the good coffee
machine at the heart of the counter and
the garish red tiles behind it. Vernasca
is, however, a very fine example of
exactly the kind of comfortable, laid-
back local caff that is most in danger.

EAST LONDON
L RODI

A long way off central London but well worth the palaver. Rodi, which has been on this site for over a century and in the hands of the same family since 1925, is a capsule of pure 1920s cockney caff. The plan is awkward, a three-room arrangement in which the middle is a converted side passage. It has a domestic scale, particularly in the rear intimate dining room. The walls of the front room present a combination of marbled green and cream Vitrolite and mirrors, with the ceiling in the same material. The old coffee machine forms the traditional counter centrepiece. A big joinery display shelf adorns the rear wall while a simple appliqué Deco clock looks down from the white wall above the counter.

The corridor which constitutes the café's spine is tiled in green and cream with black borders, with Italian travel posters and superb original bentwood coat hangers. The original pendant lampshades with glass drop shapes

survive, as do some original Deco features like the vent and the wonderfully mean serving hatch.

The rear space, however, is in a class of its own, a kind of shrine to the Italian dining room. Photos of the Rodi family and the various incarnations of the caff line the walls. The beaten Art Nouveau plated copper panels, which in the photos can be seen decorating the exterior, now hang from the walls (Breakfasts/Teas/Suppers/Dinners). An old menu card advertises 'Luigi Rodi Railway Cafe & Dining Rooms' and 'Moderate Prices' as well as listing the other three branches. The chiming, black-stained clock on the wall brings an echo of that railway association, a tinge of Brief Encounter. Rodi recalls the dining rooms which were once so ubiquitous in the capital's streets, the kind of affordable but civilised round-the-clock catering which has now all but disappeared. Catch it while you can.

E PELLICCI

The Savoy of the caff world, Pellicci's is as much essence of East End as jellied eels, the Blitz and the Krays (who were regulars here in the 1960s). Its clientele is a classic East End mix of geezers, workers, codgers and, increasingly, the arty types who have continued to move eastward over the last few years. The classes blend seamlessly here, a testament to the classic caff's genuine and broad appeal.

Pellicci's extraordinary Art Deco interior is a riot of cocktail-shaker marquetry, stained glass and sepia pictures of the old *famiglia*, in whose hands the place has been for over a century (it started off as an ice-cream parlour and current proprietor Nevio Pellicci was born upstairs). The interior is tiny and cramped, the service almost miraculously speedy (no great distances to cover) and the atmosphere consistently good-humoured and noisy.

The décor dates from just after the war, the rear end of the style: Arse Deco, we could call it. The marquetry looks like those slightly tacky Italian jewellery boxes you see at tourist shops all over Italy. The sunsets, rays and Aztec steps are one of the wonders of London's interior architecture. Check out also the terrific, almost Expressionist logo on the floor and the tiny Catholic shrine behind the counter. The café was restored after a fire in 2000 when a number of original details were lost, but the ambience and overall appearance remain unchanged. There is probably no better argument for the listing of caffs than Pellicci's robust interior. Overwhelming.

TYPOLOGY

London caff culture, even in the limited definition I have given it here, is diverse and rich. It embraces a huge number of sub-genres, some of which are covered in this book, some of which are beyond its deliberately limited scope. This very brief typology, which is entirely of my own invention but I hope will provide some familiar reference points, aims to outline a few of the more significant archetypes and to give some kind of context to the selection.

SELF-CONSCIOUS

There is a certain kind of café that has maintained its (usually 1950s) interior as a kind of attraction, an end in itself. The price of the food goes up as the interior becomes part of a marketing trick. Sausages and mash lead to the name S&M. Very clever. It may look like a caff and it is a wonderful thing that the interior has survived. But this is categorically not a caff, it is a poncey eatery. The New Piccadilly does it too.

UTILITY

During and after the Second World War a style of furniture known as utility emerged. Very unlike the Functionalism that sounds like a close cousin, utility was a blend of Victorian stuffiness, dark, unappealing materials and commercialised Art Deco, with all the fun and slickness of Paris, New York and Miami sucked clean out.

The utility caff is the catering version, often bleak and always over- or under lit, with the only decoration faded, kitschy pictures. Yet these spaces have become archetypally and indispensably London; they are spaces of tragedy, of existential angst and desolation, but also of classlessness and resistance to change, trends and corporatisation. They are such a perennial, yet modest, feature of the city's streets that they can all too easily fade into the background and become invisible. The bulk of the entries in this book come from this genre.

ICE CREAM DECO

The Italians introduced not only proper coffee to the mass market but also ice cream. The ice-cream parlours of the 1930s and 1940s were the British equivalent of American soda fountains. The kitschy Deco details, neons and pastel (or ice-cream flavour) colours were introduced from the USA, a very small touch of Hollywood on London's shabby, grey streets. The Metropolitan in Edgware Road is one of London's few survivors in this oeuvre. More and better examples can still be found in coastal resorts.

EEL AND PIE SHOPS

There is a peculiarly English, institutionalised, joyless architecture of London food that has survived in the form of the eel and pie shops that dot the capital's eastern streets. The white-tiled walls, high-backed pews and stalls and bright lighting are functional, almost municipal, and speak of an attitude to food which is to do with quick, cheap nutrition rather than a joyful, communal experience. Nevertheless many of these shops have survived incredibly intact, testifying to their appropriateness, functionality and durability. Few, if any, other commercial interiors from the Edwardian era have survived in this way. They should be cherished, even by those who are loath to eat catarrh over their pies.

CABBIES' SHELTERS

Victorian cabmen, outside in all weather and struggling to get work as there were too many of them, often resorted to booze. A bunch of philanthropists who feared for the cabmen's families and souls (and their own lives in the back of late-night cabs) built over 60 remarkable little structures in the middle of busy roads. These shelters provided hot drinks and food for cabbies throughout the night and day. Only a few have survived, with one of the best known opposite the museums in South Kensington and another by Temple station, but these mid-Victorian timber shelters are strange and wonderful survivals. The atmosphere inside is warm, comforting and excessively cosy.

SHACK

The bomb sites left in the wake of the Blitz left scores of scars in the city's urban fabric. Many of these were filled with petrol stations or garages, but some smaller plots were filled in with shoddily built shacks. Some forecourts even included little pit-stop caffs built of rendered block and roof tiles, occasionally of boarded timber. Extraordinarily, some of these have survived, often on sites too small, congested or ugly to do anything else with. There's a good one on Putney Bridge Road next to the railway viaduct.

MOSAIC CHIPPY

There is a kind of chippy that is not
really a caff, or maybe it is. The exterior
is clad in micro mosaic, the counter
serves both takeaway and café, and
the seating consists of fixed booths
with wood effect and Leatherette.
The fluorescent lighting is blinding.
The ketchup and brown sauce come
in slightly crusty, squeezy bottles.
There is a plastic fish outside and
a big jar of pickled eggs inside.
The later opening times of these
establishments have contributed
to their survival: until the arrival of
kebabs and fast food, this was all
you could get after the pub or cinema.
They still serve the same market,
thankfully.

WOOD EFFECT

A significant sub-genre of utility, the interiors of this type are enveloped in wood effect, as usually are the table tops, seating, panelling, counter fronts and sometimes even the Leatherette. Vernasca in Wentworth Street illustrates the type very well, although wood effect can also embrace a further sub-genre which takes inspiration from the brief craze for Swiss-chalet style, which hit London during the 1950s to 1960s (see the Chalet in Maddox Street) and is often seen in conjunction with nasty, spindly, wrought iron and lanterns.

KEBAB CAFF

Beyond the remit of this book, purely
due to lack of age and taste, the kebab
caffs which multiplied like Greek
rabbits across the nation's high streets
are a natural extension of the culture
established by the Mediterranean
predecessors of the Greeks, Turks and
Cypriots: the Italians. That the caffs
were mostly established in the late
1970s and 1980s, an era of low-spec,
massively over-illuminated and
hideous interiors, has not helped.
Yet they are an important part of caff
culture. Their time will come, and
by then their nasty, floor-fixed powder-
coated steel and plastic furniture
will probably have gone.

BOHO BISTRO

The Italian caff craze roughly coincided with the outbreak of the French/Italian bistro. A rash of raffia, chianti bottles, plastic ivy and rustic timber burst out across London as these new, foreign, 'sophisticated' eateries began to spread. These became existentialist student hang-outs, attractive due to their reasonable prices and their continental otherness, images of Antonioni and Godard, Gauloises and espresso.

By becoming student staples a surprising number have survived; the downstairs section of the Piccolo is a fine example, the Pollo in Soho is even better. The look is arches and Artex, dark wood and hanging junk. The boho paradise of the Troubador in Brompton Road with its dangling coffee pots and musical instruments is part of that same world.

UNDERGROUND

The huge expansion of London's Underground system in the 1930s coincided with the development of caff culture. A number of new stations incorporated little stand-up cafés or sandwich bars. Some of these retain many original features, often on the outside of the building, although the interiors tend, inevitably, to have been messed about. There's a good example at Great Portland Street and another at Stockwell. Whether stools, counter, light fittings or flooring, something has almost always survived and these little refuges humanise the transport system in a way that seems beyond current planners and designers.

TRAD ITALIAN

Real borderline this one. There are a number of long-established Italian restaurants that teeter on the edge of being caffs, with the long lists of pastas often being supplemented by English staples. I've tended to avoid these in the guide, which certainly doesn't mean they're not worth catching, just that they don't quite fit the utility aesthetic prevalent here. Among the finest examples are Dino's just around the corner from the tube in South Kensington, the Rendez Vous in Maddox Street, W1, and Lorelei in Bateman Street with its red, white and green exterior. The Pollo in Soho, with its huge menu of extraordinarily cheap and almost entirely consistently awful food, saved only by its terrific swinging London décor, is another hardy perennial. This genre, with its quaint kitschy quality, seems extremely resilient and is surviving better than the traditional workers' caff, so there's less of a hurry to see these establishments.

BIOGRAPHIES

EDWIN HEATHCOTE is an architect working and living in London. He is the architecture critic of the *Financial Times*, author of a number of books and founder of design company izé.

SUE BARR is a photographer and tutor at the Architectural Association in London. Her work has been featured in numerous international journals and publications, including *Icon* and *Architectural Design*. Her photography appears also in *Barbican: Penthouse over the City*, written by David Heathcote (Wiley-Academy, 2004).